FDR

A Life in Pictures

Compiled & Written by Michael Weishan,
President, FDR Suite Foundation,
Adams House, Harvard College

Historical Advisor — Dr. Cynthia Koch,
Public Historian in Residence, Bard College
Former Director, FDR Presidential Library
and Museum

Copyright 2013
The FDR Suite Foundation, Inc.
All rights reserved

ISBN-13: 978-1482068894
ISBN-10: 1482068893

Published by the Foundation Press
Cambridge, Massachusetts

The FDR Suite Foundation, Inc. is a 501(c)3 U.S. public charity dedicated to expanding the legacy of Franklin Delano Roosevelt and preserving the historic nature of Adams House, Harvard College, including the newly restored Franklin Delano Roosevelt Suite in Westmorly Hall.

Contributions to the Foundation are deductible to the extent allowed by law.

This book is dedicated to all those, like Franklin Roosevelt,
who not only dare dream, but dare do.

"Take a look at our present world. It is manifestly not Adolf Hitler's world. The Thousand Year Reich had a ghastly run of a dozen years. Nor is it the world of Lenin and Stalin. The Communist dream turned out to be a political, economic, and moral nightmare. Nor is it Churchill's world. He was a great war leader, but he was the son of empire, and empires have faded into oblivion. Our world today is Roosevelt's world."

Historian Arthur Schlesinger, Jr., Adams House '38

Introduction

The origins of this book are, like many I suppose, serendipitous. During visitor tours of FDR's newly restored student rooms at Adam House, I noticed that many of our guests had questions as to where, exactly, the FDR Suite stood in the grand scheme of things. Did Roosevelt have polio when he was at Harvard? Did we have pictures of the president as a student? How exactly did FDR get into politics? What were his later relations with the University? When exactly was he governor of New York? Wasn't Roosevelt also the secretary of the navy before becoming president? What about Sara? What about Eleanor…? Just enough time has passed since FDR's death in 1945 to make the general outline of events slightly fuzzy for many, so I proposed building a simple illustrated exhibit in the hallway outside the Suite to place the restoration in the larger historical context of FDR's overall life.

Simple. Yes, simple. That was the original idea. A quick, easy project. But there is nothing simple about Franklin Delano Roosevelt, his life, his family or his political career, and given that we only had ten feet of wall space to cover the events of 63 eventful years, deciding which life moments were singular enough for inclusion became an almost impossible triage. I must admit to having felt rather daunted — that is until I had another grand idea, to consult my good friend and historian Dr. Cynthia Koch, the former Director of the FDR Presidential Library and Museum at Hyde Park. Cynthia was kind enough to donate hours of her time to help me sort through the thousands of pictures available from the FDR Library, and with her help and counsel, our exhibit was born. Still, there were so many wonderful images left over, so many interesting aspects of the FDR legacy necessarily left out, that I felt strongly we ought to combine our top selections into the volume you now hold.

This book is in no way meant to be inclusive or definitive; you would need a thousand pages for that, and perhaps still fail. What it is meant to do, and what I think it uniquely succeeds in doing, is to give a real sense of the multi-faceted richness of FDR's life and times. In most of his biographies to date, illustrations are small and necessarily limited to a few pages. That's a shame, as FDR's life coincided with the great advance of photography that made it possible for the very first time to document events in actuality, rather than merely descriptively. FDR's privileged childhood comes so much more alive when he is seen dressed in his perfectly tailored riding outfit, ready for the canter; the vivaciousness of his youth is immediately evident as a strikingly handsome FDR sits at the polished wheel of his sailboat, steps off a bi-plane or whizzes across the frozen Hudson in an ice-yacht. The inexperienced first-time candidate is amusingly revealed as he peers down his pince-nez. The boy-grown-to-man standing with a newly

Warming the plush pillows of the daybed, a fire crackles in the FDR Suite hearth.

married Eleanor and — as always — mother in between, tells volumes. The travel-weary visage returning from Yalta painfully etches in place the ravages of wartime office and responsibility. The Dustbowl, the breadlines, the wheelchair, the smoke over Omaha beach: these pictures speak as no words ever could.

To this extraordinary visual chronicle we've added explanatory captions, many extended, which attempt to give the reader some sense of how each photo relates not only to FDR's life, but also to American history as a whole. Some of the images in this book have never been published; some have been published the world over; all of them are revelatory, a few extraordinarily so. None, however, are more extraordinary than the man we remember as Franklin Delano Roosevelt, and it's my hope that *FDR: A Life in Pictures* provides a suitable tribute to one of the most remarkable figures of the 20th century.

MICHAEL WEISHAN

1882

January 30th: Born in Hyde Park, New York, and seen here in his first photographic sitting with mother Sara Delano Roosevelt. Sara was the seventh of eleven Delano children and the fifth daughter born to Warren Delano II and Catherine Robbins (Lyman) Delano. The family lived at Algonac, an Italianate villa designed by Andrew Jackson Downing in Newburgh across the river from the Roosevelts. The Delanos came from old New England seafaring stock—socially prominent and immensely wealthy — which included seven members of the original Mayflower Pilgrims. Her paternal ancestor Phillippe de lay Noye was reputedly the first French Huguenot to set foot on American soil, arriving in Plymouth in 1621. FDR's grandfather, Warren Delano II, had made and lost two fortunes in the China Trade (first in tea and later in opium) before settling into the highest ranks of the New York shipping trade. Sara's upbringing was exotic: in 1862 Warren Delano brought his family to live with him in China, with Sara celebrating her eighth birthday aboard the clipper ship the *Surprise*. Her four-month voyage and the two years that followed remained the source of family pride, legend, and countless tales of the mysterious East that she later recounted to her son.

1883

At 18 months with father James Roosevelt. "Mr. James" as he was affectionately called, was a gentleman farmer. FDR's mother Sara Delano was Roosevelt's second wife; his first, Rebecca, died in 1876, having produced one son, FDR's step brother, James Roosevelt Roosevelt (known as Rosy) in 1853. The Roosevelt family traced its ancestry back to Claes Martenszen van Rosenvelt and his wife Jannetje Samuel-Thomas, who were said to have settled in New Amsterdam in about 1650, having emigrated from the village Oud-Vossameer, Zeeland, in the southwest of the Netherlands. The name Roosevelt apparently derived from that of the farm on which they lived, which must have held a "field of roses" (*rosenfeld* in Dutch). Its similarity to the name Rosenfelt gave rise in the 1930s to speculation that the Roosevelt family was originally Jewish. FDR settled the point in 1935 when he answered a reporter's question: "In the dim distant past they may have been Jews or Catholics or Protestants. What I am more interested in is whether they were good citizens and believers in God. I hope they were both." Plagued by chronic ill-health, Mr. James would die in 1900, during FDR's freshman year at Harvard.

1885

According to son Elliott, one of FDR's favorite expressions with his children was "snug as a bug in a rug" — perhaps the result of this latent memory: here our future president, age three, with the long locks that were customary for boys his age, looks entirely content to snuggle on a fur-skin rug for the photographer.

1889

FDR on his first pony, Debbie, at Hyde Park. FDR and father James enjoyed taking long rides together to inspect the various activities of the estate.

1892

By the time he was 15, it's estimated that FDR had spent seven years abroad, much of it in Europe where his ill father sought various cures. Fluent in German and French as a child, FDR is seen here at age ten in Karlsruhe, Germany practicing with his bow and arrow.

1893

Age 11, and just as his parents had wished, the aspiring country gentleman.

1897

FDR with his camera in Fairhaven, Massachusetts visiting his mother's relatives, the Delanos. The old rambling house was a favorite of FDR's, stuffed with ancient charts, nautical instruments, scrimshaw, and other mementos of entire lives spent at sea, and may have played a part in FDR's boyhood dream of joining the Navy. James and Sara wouldn't hear of it, however. Their beloved only son was destined for Groton, then Harvard, with no argument.

1899

May 27th: FDR (in the back row wearing a boater and dark jacket) as manager of the Groton baseball team after the Groton/St. Marks match. Groton won over arch-rival St. Marks, 7 to 6, in 12 innings. After the extended and hard-fought game, an enthusiastic FDR wrote to Sara: *"Well, it's all over and a more glorious victory there never has been!"* Entering in 1896, FDR spent four years at Groton. Though superficially happy in his frequent letters home, FDR, with his slight build and lack of team experience, never really fit in at a school where social distinction derived mainly from athletics, especially football. Complicating matters further was the fact that FDR's parents had been reluctant to part with their son, so he entered Groton two years later than most boys — well after schoolhouse bonds and loyalties had formed. Still, Groton, especially in the person of its Headmaster, the Reverend Endicott Peabody, left an indelible mark. FDR would remain close to Peabody for the rest of his life: Peabody would marry FDR and Eleanor, officiate at his inauguration, and supervise the education of all four Roosevelt sons.

1900

FDR's official school photo from his last year Groton.

1900

January 9th: FDR and his Groton chum Lathrop Brown ("Frank" and "Jake" to their friends) travel to Cambridge to scout rooms at their soon-to-be alma mater, Harvard: "*Then we went to the different agents & went all over the buildings, Randolph, Claverly, Russell and Westmorly. We saw many rooms, but the pick was at Westmorly, 1st floor corner looking on the South-West, and guess the price? $400 without extras... We both thought it a chance and are sure of getting it as we will be given 1st choice on Mar. 1st. On the W. side of Westmorly is Russell, then Randolph, then Claverly so all four buildings are together. The sitting room is large enough for two desks & the bedrooms and bath room are light and airy. The ceilings are very high.*" In FDR's day, the College provided housing for only 25% of its students, and most of that sub-standard rooms without central heat or hot water in the Old Yard. Students of means however, like Lathrop and FDR, were free to select lodgings in a new series of private dormitories that had arisen over the past decade along Mt. Auburn Street. Centrally heated and with modern hygienic bathrooms in each suite, these buildings offered a host of luxurious amenities. Westmorly, where FDR settled for his four years at College, was the grandest of them all: it had porter and maid service; a heated swimming pool with tropical palms; as well as a solarium on the roof. Breakfast in bed was also available — provided you rose before 11 o'clock — a feat not always attainable in an era where *soirées dansantes* commonly lasted till dawn. All this came at a rich price: the $400 rent was sufficient to feed and clothe a family of four at the turn of the last century, at a time when Harvard's tuition was $150 per year. Lathrop and FDR's first-floor rooms are visible in this period photo from the Suite's collections, precisely highlighted by the chimney shadow from the building across the street.

1901

FDR during his freshman year at Harvard, in front Springwood, his parents' home at Hyde Park, holding a dog with another at his side. Substantially remodeled and expanded in the Colonial Revival Style by FDR and Sara in 1915, Springwood would be retreat and refuge for the rest of FDR's life. Adjacent to the FDR Presidential Library and Museum, it is now managed by the National Park Service.

1901

March 29th: FDR to Sara: *"The most important news is that last night was held the election of officers of the Freshman Glee Club. President: Geo. Lawton; Secretary: F. D. Roosevelt; Gen. Manager: L. Brown. Lathrop will have to make all arrangements for the concerts of the 1904 Musical Clubs & he will have hard work. I don't have so much but have to sign the membership certificates for the whole Club."* Lathrop would add in a 1958 letter to then Adams House Master Ruben Brower: *"FDR sang 1st bass on the Freshman Glee Club (I, 2nd bass) which is part of the justification for the piano [in our rooms.]"* FDR (first row, second from left) and Lathrop (first row far right) shown here in front of Harvard's Sever Hall, were mediocre students, as was the custom of the time. Well brought up young men were discouraged from using academic achievement to show off — the famous gentleman's 'C' was the intended goal — allowing ample time for extra-curricular activities like the Freshman Glee Club.

1901

However lackluster the Harvard academic career of "Frank" and "Jake" may have been, the pair more than made up for it in the social department. Life as a "College Man" was far different from the spartan existence both had experienced at Groton. Now their weekends were filled with dances and shooting parties at suburban estates; trips to New Haven and other colleges to watch crew or football matches; overnight sleigh or carriage rides to countryside inns around Boston. For amusements of shorter duration, the two could enjoy theater evenings with the lovely Maude Adams (later of *Peter Pan* fame); social calls to families of eligible daughters like the Potters; torchlight political parades for "good ol' Cousin Ted," now President of the United States; or the famous Saturday Evening Dance Classes at the elegant Hotel Somerset. Then of course there were all the pleasant pastimes of Harvard's most elite College clubs (Lathrop the vaunted Porcellian; FDR, who was blackballed to his everlasting dismay, the less august but still posh Fly.) And, as the pair retained their luxurious lodgings in Westmorly Hall for the full four years, there was no bothersome shifting of possessions hither and thither each June and September: simply a key left with the watchful attendant, and off for a summer's sailing in Campobello or a quick trip to London on the crack new liner *Deutchland*.

1903

President of the Harvard *Crimson*, Franklin Delano Roosevelt, (front row center) with his staff. FDR fought hard to rise through the *Crimson* ranks, and even though he had technically graduated in June after only three years, (a common practice at the time) Roosevelt stayed on at the College a fourth year, primarily to become *Crimson* president. FDR considered his work on "The Crime" the highest achievement of his Harvard career, and later when in the White House often joked with the press — to their occasional consternation — about "having shared their career." He once remarked: "I must say frankly that I remember my own adventures as an editor rather more clearly than I do my routine work as a student."

1903

November 21st: The first ever Harvard-Yale game in the brand new Harvard stadium. Finished only months before, the stadium was the largest ferro-concrete structure in the world when it was built, defying skeptics who argued its huge mass would never be able to support itself. Eleanor, with Aunt Kassie and her daughter as chaperones, had traveled to Boston earlier in the day to attend "The Game." They are to be found somewhere in this picture, along with Franklin on the field, who being too slight for the Varsity, had good-naturedly volunteered to boost crowd spirit. (Franklin was an avid football fan — albeit from the sidelines — at both Groton and Harvard, and during his post on the *Crimson*, often editorialized about improving team performance.) Unfortunately FDR's cheering efforts that day were in vain: Harvard lost to Yale, 16-0.

1903

November 22nd: The day after the Harvard-Yale game, Eleanor, with Aunt and cousin still in tow, visit brother Hall at Groton. FDR, who presumably was unable to find an appropriate moment the previous day, follows Eleanor out to Groton, and proposes during a long walk down the road to the Nashoba River. At right is the very road, from a recently discovered period photo in the Suite's Lathrop Brown collection, with Groton's brand-new chapel rising in the distance. FDR had known Eleanor for years, but things only became serious after FDR pursued — and lost — Boston débutante Alice Sohier, who later confessed to a confidante that she had rejected Roosevelt because "she did not wish to be a cow," presumably a reference to FDR's desire for a large family. A week later, on Thanksgiving, he would inform his mother of his proposal to marry Eleanor. Sara stalled for time, unconvinced that her precious son was ready for marriage or correct in his choice of partner. She persuaded a reluctant FDR to wait a year before announcing their engagement — a year in which she attempted to divert FDR's affections through travel, including a cruise through the Caribbean with Sara, FDR and Lathrop Brown. But the couple held firm, and would be married in 1905.

1905

March 17th: Eleanor Roosevelt on her wedding day. The elaborate pearl and diamond necklace, aptly named a choker, was especially designed by Sara for her new daughter-in-law. By most accounts the wedding was something of a disappointment. Married at Cousin Susy's double New York City townhouse, the bride was given away by Uncle Teddy — President Theodore Roosevelt — who had sandwiched the event between two St. Patrick's Day appearances. The president swept in, gave away the bride, and swept out, taking most of the wedding guests with him. *Town Topics* later chastised "the pathetic economy" of the ceremony, noting that the food was supplied by "an Italian caterer not of the first class"; the flowers by a "Madison Avenue florist of no particular fame"; and that the narrow staircase of the home "permitted only one person to ascend or descend at a time." Furthermore Mrs. Vanderbilt was noticed to have stayed only ten minutes after the ceremony. One voice of support came from Sara. "Everyone says it was the most perfect wedding," she later wrote to FDR, "so simple and yet so elegant & refined. I was very proud of my two dear children." What attendees thought of the young couple is not recorded, though one guest was heard to remark that "the bridegroom had been especially handsome" and another had agreed, adding, "surprising for a Roosevelt."

1905

FDR and Eleanor (with mother Sara in between) soon after their marriage at the Delano estate in Newburgh, New York.

1905

Eleanor, in Venice on her second honeymoon, a photo presumably taken by FDR. Due to FDR's Columbia law school schedule, their first honeymoon had consisted of a quiet week at Hyde Park. Now with the term over, a more proper trip could be planned. After arriving in England, the Roosevelts went from London to Paris to Venice to St. Moritz and then down the Rhine — an extensive itinerary which had been personally arranged by Sara. The pair would ultimately return to the double town houses Sara was building for herself and her son on East 65th Street in New York City. The two homes would share a single entrance, and were adjoined by doors on each floor. At first Eleanor, completely untrained in domestic affairs, welcomed her mother-in-law's constant presence and advice. As the years wore on however, she began to resent the interference. But there was not much Eleanor could do to alter family dynamics: Sara controlled the Roosevelt wealth, and a chronically-short-of-cash Franklin would rely on his mother's financial assistance to fund both his family and career until her death in 1941.

1905-1909

Memories of Roosevelt as a white-haired, chair-bound president have become so ingrained in the public psyche that it's often forgotten FDR lived 39 dynamic years before contracting polio in 1921. Seen here, clockwise: at the helm of his sailboat, *Half Moon II;* golfing at his summer home in Campobello, New Brunswick; and sailing the ice yacht *Hawk* on the Hudson.

1910

November 8th: FDR is elected to the New York State Senate for Dutchess, Columbia and Putnum counties. Approached by Democratic Party officials while still practicing law in New York City, FDR jumped at the chance to represent his home district. Roosevelt tirelessly criss-crossed the three counties for weeks by the then radical means of a chauffeur-driven red Maxwell touring car. The choice of vehicle was probably not coincidental: just the year before the Maxwell had traveled over 10,000 miles of backward New England roads without stopping the motor, double the previous world record. The Maxwell possessed a particular combination of panache teamed with reliability — exactly the image of himself the newly minted candidate was hoping to project. As they bumped across field, farm, village and town, FDR stopped to talk and shake hands with practically every available voter. His enthusiasm, charm and good looks — coupled with the magic of the Roosevelt name, and, perhaps, that of the car — helped win the day: Roosevelt became the first Democrat elected in the district in 32 years. (There would not be another until 2012.) At right, a 1910 Maxwell and one of FDR's publicity pieces from the campaign.

1914

March 16th: In recognition of his support for Woodrow Wilson's presidential campaign, Roosevelt had been appointed assistant secretary of the navy in 1913. It was his preferred assignment, following in the footsteps of his distant cousin and idol, Theodore Roosevelt. Here, FDR watches the laying of keel No. 39 at the Brooklyn Navy Yard, which would later be commissioned as the U.S.S. *Arizona*. The privilege of placing the first ceremonial rivet went to three-year old Henry Williams, Jr. (son of a navy commander) who is seen clutching Roosevelt's finger. Twenty-seven years later, on December 7, 1941, now Lieutenant Henry Williams, Jr. stood on the deck of his ship at Pearl Harbor watching as the U.S.S. *Arizona* burned and sank, an ironic witness to the very moment of the ship's inception and ultimate destruction.

1915

FDR with former Groton and Harvard roommate Lathrop Brown aboard a U.S. Navy ship in Long Island Sound during FDR's term as assistant secretary. Lathrop, who served a single term in Congress in 1912, remained friends with FDR for life and later proved his staunch defender in upper-class Harvard circles where FDR's New Deal policies were wildly unpopular.

1917

Assistant Secretary of the Navy Roosevelt at rifle practice in Winthrop, Maryland. FDR was a competent shot, having been given a gun at age 11 by Mr. James — over the strenuous objections of Sara — to begin his own ornithological collection of mounted specimens. With the gun came a strict set of conditions: he could only collect one bird from each species; no birds at all from mating pairs; and all specimens to be cleaned and mounted by FDR himself. (This last was soon modified as FDR became "quite green" during early attempts to clean his birds, according to Sara, who soon allowed her son to send the kills to professional taxidermists in New York and Poughkeepsie.) FDR eventually acquired a collection that represented over 300 species of the Hudson Valley — a collection that can still be viewed today, carefully housed in glass cases at Hyde Park.

1918

In May, standing with Secretary of the Navy Josephus Daniels on the balcony of their departmental offices overlooking the White House. "You are smiling," joked Daniels, "because you are from New York and you know that someday you might live there."

1918

August 14th: Disembarking from a seaplane following an aerial inspection of naval facilities in Pauillac, France. After America's entry in WWI in 1917, FDR was anxious to enlist. President Wilson deemed his duties as assistant secretary of the navy more important, however, and Navy Secretary Josephus Daniels insisted FDR remain at his post. That summer Daniels proposed sending FDR to France ahead of a Senate inspection tour to correct anything that might attract unwanted scrutiny, and FDR extracted the promise that once his mission was completed, he be allowed to enlist. His plans were effectively short-circuited by the Spanish influenza. Returning home on the *Leviathan*, he contracted the flu complicated by pneumonia. By the time he recovered, it was obvious the war was in its final phase, and FDR remained as assistant secretary until his run for vice-president in 1920.

1919

With Eleanor, Sara, and their five surviving children from left to right: Anna (1906-1975), Franklin Jr. (1914-1988), Elliott (1910-1990) James (1907-1991), John (1916-1981). The first Franklin Jr. died an infant in 1909. This photograph, quite possibly a publicity shot for the upcoming presidential campaign, shows the full extent of the Roosevelt family. After Eleanor discovered FDR's affair with social secretary Lucy Mercer in 1918, Eleanor offered FDR a divorce. While the two were ultimately reconciled — thanks in large part to Sara who refused to even consider financially supporting a divorced son — relations between the pair were never quite the same, more of a partnership than a marriage, and almost assuredly nonsexual. Though FDR pledged never to see Lucy Mercer again, the two remained affectionate friends at a distance, and after 1940 would occasionally meet for a drive or quiet dinner at the White House when Eleanor was away — with FDR's daughter Anna acting as hostess. Ironically, it was Lucy Mercer (along with two other female friends), not Eleanor, who was with FDR when he died at Warm Springs.

1919

FDR (in brimmed hat) next to President Wilson (in profile) aboard the SS *George Washington*, returning from France. Roosevelt, who had just finished a postwar mission to dispose of U.S. Navy assets in Europe, had joined Wilson for the voyage home from the Paris peace conference. The original intention was for the *George Washington* to dock in New York, but once underway, the president changed his mind and instructed the captain to land in Boston where Wilson was scheduled to make a speech introducing the League of Nations. The captain, to his dismay, found that the ship carried no charts for Boston Harbor and was forced to navigate the last part of the voyage by dead reckoning. A thick fog descended as the ship approached the Massachusetts shore, and the *George Washington* narrowly avoided coming to grief off the rocks of Nahant, a popular summer colony north of Boston. FDR, awakened from his bed by the shuddering sound of engines in emergency reverse, rushed to the bridge, recognized the fog-bound coast from his youthful sails there, and was able to direct the captain safely to Boston Harbor. According to FDR's own account, Wilson slept soundly through the entire affair and was never even aware how close to disaster the ship had come.

1920

The election of 1920 was dominated by the aftermath of World War I and a backlash against the progressive politics of President Wilson. During the past year, the wartime economic boom had collapsed. Veterans returned home to find few jobs and general unrest. Major strikes occurred in the meatpacking and steel industries. Anarchist mail bombs directed at prominent government officials killed one and severely damaged several homes and offices. Large-scale race riots broke out in Chicago and other cities. A terrorist attack on Wall Street in September 1919, which killed 38, exacerbated fears that the country was falling into Communist-led anarchy. From the White House came little guidance: Wilson's leadership ability was critically weakened after he suffered a severe stroke that October that rendered him unable to speak. The Democrats, meeting in San Francisco, nominated a newspaper editor from Ohio, Governor James M. Cox, (at left) as their presidential candidate; 38-year-old Franklin D. Roosevelt was chosen as his running mate. That November, Republican Warren Harding won with a landslide 60% of the popular vote and 404 votes in the Electoral College — the largest popular percentage since 1820. Despite the fact that Cox was defeated badly, FDR became a well-known political figure thanks to his active and energetic campaign.

1924

In 1921 at the age of 39, FDR developed acute symptoms of poliomyelitis while at his summer home on Campobello Island. It is believed that he was infected while visiting a Boy Scout encampment at Bear Mountain State Park, New York, on July 28. Despite years of physical therapy, FDR never walked again. He had to be carried when transferred from place to place and employed a wheelchair when moving about in private quarters. FDR found the buoyant mineral waters at Warm Springs, Georgia helpful to his therapy and in 1926 invested most of his resources in the purchase of a run-down resort, which he converted into a national rehabilitation center for polio victims. The March of Dimes evolved out of Roosevelt's fundraising efforts for the Warm Springs Foundation, which is credited with funding the research that led to the polio vaccine in the 1950s. FDR maintained a cottage at Warm Springs known as "The Little White House," and it was there that he died on April 12, 1945. Here, FDR is seen on crutches posing for the press with 1924 Democratic presidential candidate John W. Davies. Realizing that crutches were a political liability, he laboriously learned to project the appearance of walking by precariously balancing himself on leg braces, canes and the support of his son or an aide.

1928

Despite his illness, FDR kept an active interest in politics during the 1920s. Eleanor and his political advisor Louis Howe maintained Democratic Party contacts and made sure his name stayed before the press. When New York Governor Al Smith decided to run for president against Herbert Hoover in 1928, the Party turned to Roosevelt to fill his seat. Roosevelt was reluctant on two counts. By now he was very much involved with the day-to-day running of his Warm Springs Foundation, and wished to continue. Equally, he and political advisor Louis Howe felt Democratic prospects extremely dim in the buoyant economy of 1928, preferring to defer any potential run until 1932. Assurances of financial backing for his Foundation during his absence, and all-out political support from New York State Democrats, combined to change his mind. FDR had, however, been right about the mood: in November Al Smith lost in a landslide, but thanks to a highly efficient campaign, Roosevelt squeaked out a 25,000 vote victory, with over four million votes cast. He was now Governor of New York.

1929

During the later half of the 1920s, the American economy boomed, often outperforming the previous year by 20% or more. Such growth created a surge of stock exchange speculation that sent hundreds of thousands of Americans to invest heavily in the market for the first time. By August 1929, brokers were routinely lending small investors money to buy stock — as much as 80% of the purchase price. The result was a tower of debt: more than $8.5 billion in loans was outstanding, an amount which exceeded the entire amount of currency circulating in the U.S. at the time. On October 28th and 29th, the market crashed, forcing margin calls across the country. Thousands were bankrupted overnight, and millions ultimately lost their jobs. Though not the sole cause of what would become known as the Great Depression, the crash was a primary contributor, and began a period of economic malaise that would last most of the 1930s, until the onset of massive government spending during World War II. The market, however, would not return to its 1929 peak until 1954.

1932

As Governor, Roosevelt at first proposed standard progressive projects like rural electrification and agricultural reform, but after the 1929 stock market crash, an increasingly concerned FDR pressed for more radical action. He authorized a commission to stabilize employment in New York State, and was the first state chief executive to endorse unemployment insurance. A worried public agreed, easily returning FDR to the governor's chair in 1930. In August, responding to the continuing economic free-fall, FDR proposed the first-ever statewide program of public relief: TERA, the Temporary Emergency Relief Administration, which became a nationwide model. This program marked a turning point in FDR's thinking, and was the genesis of what would later become the New Deal. At right, the famous White Angel Breadline photo of Dorothea Lange captures the desperation of a nation.

1932

FDR, who was never fond of flying, radiates confidence from the window of a chartered Ford Tri-motor, awaiting refueling in Cleveland while on the way to the Democratic Convention in Chicago. FDR's decision to arrive by airplane — the first presidential candidate ever to do so and the first to attend his own nominating convention — electrified the country in an age when aviation was in its romantic infancy and the set the tone of progress that would embody his campaign for the presidency. The Tri-motor pictured here in a dramatically lit night scene comes from a period advertisement in the Suite's collection.

1932

The selection of the song that would become forever associated with FDR and the Democrats — "Happy Days Are Here Again" — was entirely fortuitous. The former assistant naval secretary had somewhat predictably chosen "Anchors Away" as his campaign song, but its continual reprise awaiting the candidate's dramatic arrival at the Democratic Convention in Chicago so wearied Roosevelt's chief political advisor Louis Howe that he demanded the band play something, anything else. When asked what, Howe recalled a tune a secretary of his had been humming earlier. It turned out to be a catchy little number from the 1930 MGM all-talkie *Chasing Rainbows,* which had otherwise been an altogether forgettable box office flop. (So much so, in fact, that the rare two-strip Technicolor finale sequence which introduced the song was cut from the eventual re-release and has now been completely lost.) "Oh tell 'em to play 'Happy Days are Here Again,'" he instructed, never realizing he had just immortalized an anthem for FDR and the New Deal.

1932

Never one to miss a good photo opportunity, — and certainly unaware of Native American sensibilities — "Chief" Roosevelt dons a Plains Indian headdress at Ten Mile River Boy Scout camp at Dover, New York during the campaign. FDR had a genuine love of scouting, and would be the first active Scout leader to reach the White House. In 1934, hundreds of thousands of Scouts would respond to Roosevelt's broadcast appeal to help the needy, collecting nearly two million articles of clothing, household furnishings, and other items for poor families. The president would maintain close ties to the Scouts for the rest of his life.

1932

. . . Here I was, in a country where a right to say how the country should be governed was restricted to six persons in each thousand of its population. . . I was become a stockholder in a corporation where nine hundred and ninety-four of the members furnished all the money and did all the work, and the other six elected themselves a permanent board of direction and took all the dividends. It seemed to me that what the nine hundred and ninety-four dupes needed was a new deal.
Mark Twain: A Connecticut Yankee in King Arthur's Court

Borrowing Twain's phrase (as the *New York Times* alleged), FDR had promised a "New Deal" for the American people in his nomination speech, and hammered this message home on trips across the country, like here, aboard the "Roosevelt Express." The pledge resonated with a fearful nation: FDR carried all but six states against the incumbent Republican president, Herbert Hoover, winning the Electoral College 472 to 59. He would inherit a country in crisis. By the time he assumed office in March 1933, the national overall unemployment rate would be 25%; the manufacturing unemployment rate 35%; the construction rate 75%. The year would see millions homeless as riots broke out in cities and rural areas as families lost their farms and homes to foreclosure. Local charities were simply overwhelmed as the crisis threatened to irreparably rend the nation's social and economic fabric.

1933

On the day after his March 4th inauguration, Roosevelt declared a Bank Holiday, allowing for stabilization of the nation's banks – two-thirds of which were already closed. Passage of the Emergency Banking Act on March 9th, followed by the Securities Act and the Glass-Steagall Banking Act (which included the FDIC) are widely credited with preserving the nation's financial system. Speaking to the nation on the radio March 12th to explain his policies in the first of his famous "Fireside Chats," Roosevelt began simply: *"I want to talk for a few minutes with the people of the United States about banking… I want to tell you what has been done in the last few days, why it was done, and what the next steps are going to be."* FDR would ultimately have more than 30 of these folksy, easy-to-understand talks with the American people, which for the first time used the airwaves to define a direct relationship between the presidency and the electorate.

BANK HOLIDAYS
March 6, 7, 8 and 9, 1933
By Proclamation of the President of the United States of America

No Business Will Be Transacted on These Days

SAFE DEPOSIT VAULTS OPEN AS USUAL

1933

In his first hundred days, in addition to reforms of the banking and security industries, FDR won congressional passage for an unprecedented series of relief and progressive reform measures. The Federal Emergency Relief Administration, supplied states and localities with emergency money to provide jobs (rather than the "dole") for the unemployed. The Agricultural Adjustment Act provided comprehensive farm relief. The Public Works Administration focused on creating jobs through infrastructure development in such areas as water systems, power plants, and hospitals. The Civilian Conservation Corps, whose members are seen here transplanting young trees in Oregon's Mt. Shasta National Park, provided jobs for hundreds of thousands of unemployed young men. The Tennessee Valley Authority boosted regional development. The Farm Credit Act and the Home Owners' Loan Act extended much-needed credit and the National Recovery Act (later overturned) proposed to regulate business and industry. In all, Roosevelt succeeding in passing 15 major bills in his first hundred days that used the power of federal government to restore confidence and raise the morale of the nation. "Congress doesn't pass legislation anymore—they just wave at the bills as they go by," noted humorist Will Rogers.

1933

March 22nd: One of the most popular results of the first hundred days was the Beer–Wine Revenue Act. The bill, which had been a plank in the Democratic platform of 1932, permitted the sale of beer and wine with an alcohol content of less than 3.2% by volume, and brought relief to a restive country weary of Prohibition. The Twenty-first Amendment would fully restore drinkers' rights on December 5th.

1933

June 16th: Sailing from Marion, Massachusetts to Campobello New Brunswick aboard the *Amberjack II* at the end of the soon-to-be famous "hundred days." This was FDR's first trip back to the island since he contracted polio in 1921, and he piloted the boat the entire 400-mile voyage by dead reckoning — a remarkable feat. Gone, however, were the quiet sails of his youth. The chartered *Amberjack II* with the President of the United States on board was trailed by two destroyers, three coast guard cutters, two press boats, and the heavy cruiser USS *Indianapolis*. "I am having a bang-up good time, and I do not intend to go ashore anywhere along the coast," he told reporters. "This is my vacation, and I am going to stay aboard this boat the whole two weeks." After terrorizing the Secret Service by sailing through squalls, high seas, and fog (without a radio), FDR and his small crew arrived at Friar's Head dock on Campobello June 29th for a four-day stay on the island. He would return to his boyhood summer home only twice more, in 1936 and 1939.

1934

Jan 30th: An essential to being part of FDR's personal coterie was the ability to laugh, and especially, to laugh at oneself. Here, the Cuff Links Gang, originally an all-male group of the president's longtime friends and advisors but later expanded to include both sexes, celebrate "Caesar's" birthday, a not-too-veiled reference to FDR's political critics who compared him to a dictator. Thanks in no small part to FDR's sage policies, this playful romp is as close as America ever came to fascist leadership in the 1930s.

1934-1936

In the 1920s extensive mechanized plowing of virgin topsoil in the Great Plains destroyed the native deep-rooted grasses that held the soil. During a natural drought cycle in the 30s, without these grass anchors to keep the earth in place, the newly opened fields dried, turned to dust, and blew away with the prevailing winds. At times, enormous dust clouds blackened the sky, reaching all the way to New York and Washington D.C. These immense storms — given names such as "black blizzards" and "black rollers" — often reduced visibility to a few feet or less, completely burying the landscape in their aftermath. The Dust Bowl affected 100,000,000 acres centered on the panhandles of Texas and Oklahoma, and adjacent parts of New Mexico, Colorado, and Kansas, displacing vast segments of the population. Under FDR, modern farming and conservation practices were mandated that eventually mitigated the situation. The famous image of a mother and her two children by New Deal Farm Security Administration photographer Dorothea Lange (upper right) summarizes the poverty and desperation of those who fled the Dust Bowl seeking a better life in the West.

1935

Americans often forget that the legacy of the New Deal still actively shapes our physical environment today via a vast body of public works. The number and extent of these New Deal-sponsored projects are staggering, dotting the country from coast to coast: libraries, courthouses, bridges, waterworks, roads, parks, gardens, public artwork, post offices — even airports. Three of the most famous, National (now Reagan) Airport in Washington DC, La Guardia in New York, and LAX in Los Angeles have their founding in New Deal initiatives. FDR took particular pleasure in personally dedicating these works, and is seen here in September, driving through a portion of Boulder (Hoover) Dam.

1935

The economics of the Depression were particularly devastating for older Americans. In 1870 over 70% of elderly males were reported as gainfully employed, mostly in farming. Due to shifting demographics and increased urbanization, by 1930 the figure had dropped to 33% (8% for women) with drastic results. Age discrimination and bias were rampant in the workforce, and what little employment was available went to younger men. Homelessness and starvation loomed for many elderly. Emboldened to act, FDR and Secretary of Labor Frances Perkins proposed a joint federal-state system for old-age assistance, which was ultimately expanded to cover unemployment insurance, aid to the blind, and aid to dependent mothers and children. The linchpin to this social security system was a payroll tax. Although controversial, FDR insisted taxation, rather than appropriation, be the principal finance mechanism for the program: "We put those payroll contributions there," he said, "so as to give the contributors a legal, moral and political right to collect their pensions and their unemployment benefits. With those taxes in there, no damn politician can ever scrap my social security program." The social security program remains the principal means of governmental support for elderly Americans to this day.

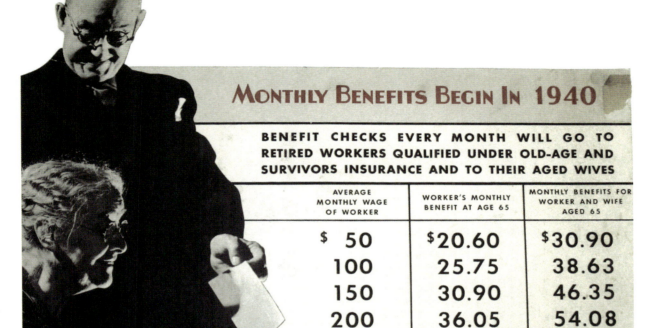

1936

With classmate Grenville Clark '04 at Harvard's 300th Anniversary celebration on a cold, wet September day. Despite having been awarded an honorary degree while Governor of New York, and having served as a Harvard Overseer, FDR's relations with his alma mater were often rocky. Roosevelt had been invited to speak by Harvard's president emeritus, A. Lawrence Lowell, who was no fan of FDR, and who began by suggesting that the occasion would be an "opportunity to divorce yourself from the arduous demands of politics and political speech-making," adding that "it would be well to limit all the speeches that afternoon to about ten minutes." FDR wrote to an advisor, "I felt like replying: 'If I am invited in my capacity as a Harvard graduate I shall, of course, speak as briefly as you suggest — two minutes if you say so — but if I am invited as president to speak for the nation, I am unable to tell you at this time what my subject will be or whether it will take five minutes or an hour!'" At the ceremony, FDR deliberately omitted Lowell's name from his opening salutation and began jauntily by reminding his listeners that "*The roots of Harvard are deep in the past. It is pleasant to remember today that this meeting is being held in pursuance of an adjournment expressly taken 100 years ago on motion of Josiah Quincy. At that time many of the alumni of Harvard were sorely troubled concerning the state of the nation. Andrew Jackson was president. On the 250th anniversary of the founding of Harvard College, alumni again were sorely troubled. Grover Cleveland was president. Now, on the 300th anniversary, I am president....*" His eloquent speech did, in fact, come in at just under ten minutes.

1936

November 16th: The president reviews the Argentine fleet during a trip to South America aboard the USS *Indianapolis*. Roosevelt had announced in his first inaugural address that he "would dedicate this nation to the policy of the good neighbor." Expanding on this theme at the Pan American Conference in Uruguay in 1933, FDR pledged the United States to be respectful and friendly in its relations with other nations of the Western Hemisphere, which came to be coined the "Good Neighbor Policy." In practical terms this meant the withdrawal of US forces in Haiti; the elimination of restrictive tariffs on Cuba; a new treaty with Panama that removed some of the inequalities of earlier agreements; and the establishment of a hemispheric security zone which proved a powerful bulwark against the rapidly decaying political situation in Europe. Sadly, the *Indianapolis,* which carried Roosevelt three times during his presidency and later became flagship of the 5th Fleet, scarcely outlived her proud commander-in-chief. Torpedoed by the Japanese in July, 1945, the ship rolled upside down and sank in 12 minutes. Some 300 trapped sailors went directly to the bottom. The 900 remaining crew were dumped into shark infested waters with few lifeboats. Though distress calls had been transmitted before the *Indianapolis* foundered, they were inexplicably disregarded by naval radio operators. The sinking was only discovered during a routine patrol flight four days later, by which time 317 crewmen remained alive — the greatest single loss of life at sea in the history of the U.S. Navy.

1936

Eleanor Roosevelt visits a WPA school for black children in Des Moines. Though both Eleanor and FDR were personally sympathetic to the plight of African Americans, the Roosevelt Administration's record on civil rights is not stellar. This was due mostly to a block of highly conservative Southern Democratic senators ready to withhold support from any measure that smacked of reform. Simply put, Roosevelt needed Southern support to pass his legislative agenda, and the price was FDR's inaction on civil rights. FDR actively chafed at this control, and attempted in the election of 1938 to work to defeat some of his most conservative opponents in the South. With a few exceptions, this policy backfired and FDR was forced to back down. Later, in 1944, Roosevelt even went so far as to consider the formation of a new third "progressive" party with his former 1940 Presidential opponent Wendell Willkie, but with war raging in Europe, the idea went nowhere. Civil rights would have to wait another 20 years for any true progress.

1937

March: Eleanor Roosevelt, in the gown she wore to FDR's second inauguration. The 1936 election was a resounding victory for Roosevelt, the New Deal and the Democratic Party. Roosevelt lost only two states, Maine and Vermont, and amassed 523 electoral votes to Republican Alfred Landon's eight. He won an overwhelming 60.8% of the popular vote and Democrats controlled both houses of Congress by wide margins. The 1936 election marked the beginning of the New Deal coalition of the white working class, blacks, the Deep South, and northern intellectuals that would dominate the Democratic party for generations.

1937

Flush from his resounding electoral victory and faced with a highly conservative Supreme Court that had rolled back several major New Deal initiatives, Roosevelt worried that Social Security and the Wagner Act (National Labor Relations Act) would be overturned by the "Nine Old Men" in 1937. On the pretense of improving efficiency, he proposed to increase the size of the Supreme Court (and the federal judiciary) by nominating a new justice every time an existing jurist reached the age of 70 and did not resign or retire within six months. Under his plan, the president could appoint as many as 44 new federal judges and six new Supreme Court justices. While the actual number of Supreme Court justices is not constitutionally fixed and has historically varied from five to ten — Congress has altered the constitution of the Court six times, often for blatantly political purposes — FDR's attempt took the nation by surprise and became known as the "Court-packing Plan." Actions by the Court itself ultimately derailed the scheme before it reached an uncertain vote in Congress. Conservative Justice Owen Roberts unexpectedly voted to uphold New Deal legislation and Justice Willis Vandevanter, an opponent of the expansion of the authority of the federal government, retired.

1939

May 17th: The German liner *St. Louis* attempts to dock in Havana harbor, with 937 souls on board, mostly Jews fleeing Nazi persecution. Though passengers had obtained landing permits before sailing, the Cuban government, bowing to antisemitic pressure and charges of corruption in the visa process, had retroactively canceled these permits on May 5th. Despite diplomatic pressure from the U.S. Secretary of State Cordell Hull, and Henry Morgenthau, Secretary of the Treasury, the Cuban government refused to allow the majority of Jewish passengers to disembark. After days of fruitless negotiations, the captain then turned the ship towards Miami, with the hope that the United States would accept the passengers. Though personal appeals were made to FDR, the president chose not to intervene, allowing Hull and Morganthau (who was Jewish) to successfully negotiate with England, France, Belgium and the Netherlands to accept the immigrants. The *St. Louis* returned to Europe, arriving at Antwerp June 17th, where the passengers finally disembarked. Some historians have accused FDR of blatant antisemitism in refusing the passengers, which is inaccurate. The real problem lay with the strict (and racially motivated) quotas established in the U.S. Immigration and Nationality Act of 1924 that limited the number of immigrants who could be admitted from any one country. In 1939, the annual combined German-Austrian immigration quota was 27,370 and had been quickly filled, with a waiting list of at least several years. Allowing the *St. Louis* passengers to the head of the line would have merely bumped an equivalent number of already approved immigrants off the list. With the economy still mired in the Depression (unemployment was running at 17%), an isolationist American electorate was in no mood to help foreigners while so many fellow-citizens were still in need. The compromise Secretary Hull worked out would have proved perfectly viable — had the Nazis not done the unthinkable and overrun Western Europe six months later. Ultimately 227 of the passengers who settled on the Continent would perish in German death camps.

1939

England's King George VI, the first British Monarch to visit the United States, with FDR. The visit, which lasted five days in June, ended at Hyde Park, where, much to the horror of FDR's mother Sara, Eleanor served the King and Queen of England hot dogs on the front porch of Top Cottage. (They were delighted, according to the Queen, finding the Roosevelts "a charming and united family and living so like English people when they come to their country house.") The visit of the King and Queen three months before the outbreak of the war in Europe did much to cement the goodwill of the American public towards Britain and would prove to be of incalculable value to the later Allied war effort.

1939

September 3rd: Roosevelt addresses the people of the United States after Germany invades Poland:

"This nation will remain a neutral nation, but I cannot ask that every American remain neutral in thought as well. Even a neutral has a right to take account of facts. Even a neutral cannot be asked to close his mind or his conscience. I have said not once, but many times, that I have seen war and that I hate war. I say that again and again. I hope the United States will keep out of this war. I believe that it will. And I give you assurance and reassurance that every effort of your Government will be directed toward that end. As long as it remains within my power to prevent, there will be no black-out of peace in the United States."

1940

When FDR decided to run for an unprecedented third term, Republican opponent Wendell Willkie crusaded against Roosevelt's attempt to break the two-term presidential tradition, arguing that "if one man is indispensable, then none of us is free." Even some Democrats agreed, and Willkie hoped to attract substantial Democratic support with posters like the one at right. However the war raging in Europe convinced many that it was not the time to "change horses in mid-stream." After France fell and Hitler's bombs pounded Britain into the summer and fall, even Willkie came to share Roosevelt's view that it was necessary to aid Britain materially in its war against the Nazis — short of entering a "shooting war" by using American troops — which weakened the isolationist debate. Though he won a lower percentage of the popular vote (54.7%) than he had in his two previous runs, FDR swept the electoral college 449-82 to easily win a third term. In a classic pose, FDR is seen below right during the campaign that September speaking at the dedication ceremony for the Great Smoky Mountains National Park.

1940

The undamaged dome of St. Paul's Cathedral stands out among the flames and smoke during firebombing by the German Luftwaffe on December 29th. Following the fall of France in June, Great Britain stood alone at war against Nazi Germany. The United States, still staunchly isolationist, refused to take sides, forcing Britain to pay for its war matériel in gold under a "cash and carry" policy as required by the Neutrality Acts. Throughout the long presidential campaign that year, British Prime Minister Winston Churchill had repeatedly pressed FDR for American help, as a desperate Great Britain had liquidated so many assets that it was running short of cash. After the election in November, Churchill again appealed to Roosevelt, who was now in a position to take action. Still hampered by the Neutrality Acts, Roosevelt devised the ingenious idea of Lend-Lease, which "loaned" war materials to be used "until time for their return or destruction." Many Republicans were skeptical: Robert Alphonso Taft, Senator from Ohio, responded: "Lending war equipment is a good deal like lending chewing gum. You don't want it back." Formally entitled *An Act to Further Promote the Defense of the United States*, Lend-Lease — along with the first-ever peacetime draft — moved the nation toward the seemingly inevitable conflict with Germany.

1941

February: On the porch of Top Cottage at Hyde Park, New York, with his caretaker's granddaughter, Ruthie Bie, and his beloved Scottie, Fala. This photograph, a private snap taken by his friend, Margaret "Daisy" Suckley, is one of the very few existing pictures showing FDR in his wheelchair.

1941

December 7th: The U.S.S. *Arizona* — the same ship FDR helped launch in 1914 — burning at Pearl Harbor. In his "Day of Infamy" speech to Congress December 8th, FDR asked for and received a declaration of war against Japan. The other two Axis powers — following the terms of the 1940 Tripartite Pact, which pledged Germany, Italy and Japan to "stand by and co-operate with one another in . . . their prime purpose to establish and maintain a new order of things" — declared war on the United States on December 11th.

1942

February 19th: Roosevelt signs Executive Order 9066 authorizing military officials to exclude "any and all persons" from areas of the U.S. mainland designated as "military zones." Although no specific ethnic group was mentioned, the order gave the military the authority to intern people who were seen as potential threats — some Germans and Italians in the East, but mainly Japanese on the West Coast. It was followed in March by Congressional legislation to enforce the decree with criminal penalties. By the end of the year, 110,000 Japanese Americans — two-thirds of them U.S. citizens — would be rounded up and placed into internment camps in inland areas, away from the potential war zone in Pacific coastal areas. The average duration of their captivity would be 900 days. Roosevelt was responding not only to the public hysteria in the aftermath of Pearl Harbor, but also to recommendations from advisors at all levels of government. Canada and 12 Latin American countries enacted similar legislation. Eleanor Roosevelt opposed internment, as did key members of the Roosevelt Administration, especially attorneys at the Justice Department and the F.B.I., who argued that the order was both illegal and unnecessary. These objections were overruled, and in the few test cases that ultimately reached the Supreme Court during the war, the Government's action was upheld, the justices deciding that the war powers granted to the president outweighed due process and equal protection claims. In retrospect, it is clear that the Japanese internment during WWII was racially motivated. In 1983 a Congressional commission set up to review the wartime record found that the evidence the Government presented to the Supreme Court had been tainted and that "race prejudice, war hysteria, and failure of political leadership had resulted in grave injustice to Japanese-Americans."

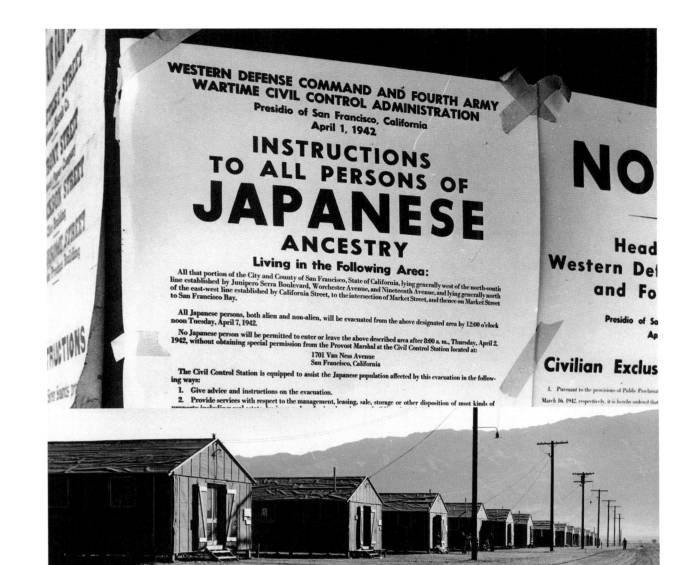

1942

WWII transformed life on the home front in countless ways. With critical raw materials needed for armaments, production of non-essential civilian goods such a new cars and refrigerators ceased early in the year. Americans would simply have to do without for the duration, and with each new address, FDR urged his fellow Americans to redouble their energies toward victory. Scrap metal and spare rubber drives became frequent activities, and resulted in millions of tons of material for the war effort. Methods of food production changed too: with a 17% reduction in the farm population, commercial agriculture was forced to streamline operations in order to feed the troops abroad. Domestic rationing and price controls were implemented for many commodities, and home "victory" gardens were encouraged to fill the gap. Urged on by government posters like this one, these gardening efforts were amazingly productive. By the end of the war it was estimated that close to 40% of produce consumed in the U.S. originated in backyard gardens.

1943

The Boeing Renton plant in Washington State producing B-29 Super Fortresses. Unemployment, which had been as high as 17.2% in 1939, fell to 1.2% in 1944, as war production quickly ended the Depression. "Rosie the Riveter" was more than a popular song: for the first time women and minorities entered into the manufacturing workforce in large numbers, changing forever the face of the American workplace.

1943

FDR reviewing the troops in Rabat, Morocco, while at the Casablanca Conference. Roosevelt was the first U.S. president to travel by plane, and the first to travel outside the United States during war time: to the international Allied conferences in Casablanca (1943), Quebec I (1943), Tehran (1943), Quebec II (1944) and Yalta (1945), as well as his Inspection Tour of the Pacific (Hawaii and Alaska) in 1944.

1943

The first meeting of the "Big Three" — Roosevelt, Stalin and Churchill — at the Tehran Conference, which committed the Allies to open a second front against Nazi Germany. The conference also addressed relations between the Allies and Turkey and Iran, operations in Yugoslavia, and against Japan, as well as the envisaged post-war settlement of Europe.

1944

With the nation at war, FDR chose to run again for an unheard of fourth term against his Republican opponent, the Governor of New York, Thomas E. Dewey. FDR's dog, Fala, became an issue in the campaign when Republicans accused FDR of sending a destroyer to retrieve the pooch who, they charged, had been accidentally left behind during a presidential tour of the Pacific. FDR rebutted the charge in his famous "Fala speech":

"These Republican leaders have not been content with attacks on me, or my wife, or on my sons. No, not content with that, they now include my little dog, Fala. Well, of course, I don't resent attacks, and my family doesn't resent attacks, but Fala does resent them. You know, Fala is Scotch, and being a Scottie, as soon as he learned that the Republican fiction writers in Congress and out had concocted a story that I had left him behind on the Aleutian Islands and had sent a destroyer back to find him - at a cost to the taxpayers of two or three, or eight or twenty million dollars- his Scotch soul was furious. He has not been the same dog since. I am accustomed to hearing malicious falsehoods about myself - such as that old, worm-eaten chestnut that I have represented myself as indispensable. But I think I have a right to resent, to object to, libelous statements about my dog."

The uproarious laughter that followed these remarks was symbolic: FDR won the election 432 electoral votes to 99 with 53.4% of the popular vote. Here, a canine supporter, albeit one with a slight spelling problem, carries an election sign.

1944

June 6th: American soldiers land on Omaha Beach under heavy Nazi machine gun fire, to begin the assault on Hitler's "Fortress Europe." There is a tendency today to remember Roosevelt primarily as a domestic president, the grand proponent of the New Deal, but Roosevelt himself was even prouder of his role as Commander-in- Chief, going so far as to instruct his cabinet to address him as such rather than Mr. President after the outbreak of WWII. As a war leader, Roosevelt became much more involved in planning and strategy than had any other president before him, essentially relegating the War and Navy departments to administrative duties after his formation of the Joint Chiefs in 1942. While he relied heavily on their judgment, he was not afraid to overrule the Chiefs, having formed considerable confidence in his own strategic abilities. All in all he would countermand the advice of his generals 22 times: the invasion of northwest Africa in 1942; the policy of unconditional surrender announced at Casablanca in 1943; and his recall of general Stilwell from the China-Burma-India theater in 1944 are but several examples. It was FDR, too, who appointed Dwight D. Eisenhower over higher ranking generals to run the Normandy invasion. The consensus of historians is that FDR was correct in his military judgment more often than not. His vigorous leadership, despite increasingly severe health issues, was critical to the ultimate success of the military effort and the primary factor that kept alive the fragile coalition that ultimately defeated Germany and Japan.

1945

February 4-11th: The Yalta Conference. For the second time FDR meets with Winston Churchill and Josef Stalin. The conference, convened near Yalta, in the Crimea, was intended to formulate plans for reconstructing the nations of war-torn Europe. With the war still raging in the Pacific, FDR sought to secure Stalin's commitment to enter what was predicted to be an bloody island-by-island campaign against Japan. A few years later, with the Cold War dividing the globe, Yalta would become a subject of intense controversy, some arguing that a visibly tired and weakened FDR was overly trusting of Russian promises to allow free elections in Eastern Europe — elections which subsequently never occurred. Supporters would argue that Roosevelt's detractors overlooked the ardent desire of the Joint Chiefs to secure Russian participation against Japan, as well as the then dominant position of the Soviet Army in Eastern Europe. Of course, none of the participants could know that the Pacific War would come to a rapid and dramatic end with the dropping of the atomic bombs on Nagasaki and Hiroshima later that August.

1945

April 11th: The last photograph of President Roosevelt, taken at his cottage at Warm Springs, Georgia by Nicholas Robbins for Elizabeth Shoumatoff, who was painting a portrait of the president.

1945

April 12th: A nation mourns.

The New York Times.

LATE CITY EDITION

VOL. XCIV...No. 31,856. NEW YORK, FRIDAY, APRIL 13, 1945. THREE CENTS

PRESIDENT ROOSEVELT IS DEAD; TRUMAN TO CONTINUE POLICIES; 9TH CROSSES ELBE, NEARS BERLIN

U. S. AND RED ARMIES DRIVE TO MEET

Americans Across the Elbe in Strength Race Toward Russians Who Have Opened Offensive From Oder

WEIMAR TAKEN, RUHR POCKET SLASHED

Third Army Reported 19 Miles From Czechoslovak Border—British Drive Deeper in the North, Seizing Celle—Canadians Freeing Holland

By DREW MIDDLETON

PARIS, April 12—Thousands of tanks and a half million doughboys of the United States First, Third and Ninth Armies are racing through the heart of the Reich on a front of 150 miles, threatening Berlin, Leipzig and the last citadels of the Nazi power.

The Second Armored Division of the Ninth Army has crossed the Elbe River in force and is striking eastward toward Berlin, whose outskirts lie less than sixty miles to the east, according to reports from the front. [A report quoted by The United Press placed the Americans less than fifty miles from the capital.] Beyond Berlin the First White Russian Army has crossed the Oder on a wide front and a junction between the western and eastern Allies is not far off.

[The Moscow radio reported that heavy battles were raging west of the Oder before Berlin, indicating that Marshal Gregory K. Zhukoff has launched his drive toward the Reich's capital. The Soviet communiqué announced further progress by the Red Army forces in and around Vienna.]

Paris is wild with excitement to— A special edition of the newspaper France-Soir carries a report by the radio station "Voice of America" that places American forces fifteen and five-eighths miles from Berlin after an air landing that had linked up with Lieut. Gen. William H. Simpson's forces advancing eastward on the Elbe. This would put American forces only seventy-five

OUR OKINAWA GUNS DOWN 118 PLANES

Japanese Fliers Start 'Suicide' Attacks on Fleet, Sink a Destroyer, Hit Other Ships

By W. H. LAWRENCE

GUAM, Friday, April 13—Japanese attempting to halt the American march to Tokyo, have started "desperate, suicidal" aerial attacks upon our ships and men in the Okinawa area, losing 118 planes on Thursday alone, Fleet Admiral

Franklin Delano Roosevelt
1882-1945

END COMES SUDDENLY AT WARM SPRINGS

Even His Family Unaware of Condition as Cerebral Stroke Brings Death to Nation's Leader at 63

ALL CABINET MEMBERS TO KEEP POSTS

Funeral to Be at White House Tomorrow, With Burial at Hyde Park Home— Impact of News Tremendous

By ARTHUR KROCK

WASHINGTON, April 12—Franklin Delano Roosevelt, War President of the United States and the only Chief Executive in history who was chosen for more than two terms, died suddenly and unexpectedly at 4:35 P. M. today at Warm Springs, Ga., and the White House announced his death at 5:48 o'clock. He was 63.

The President, stricken by a cerebral hemorrhage, passed from unconsciousness to death on the eighty-third day of his fourth term and in an hour of high triumph. The armies and fleets under his direction as Commander in Chief were at the gates of Berlin and on the shores of Japan's home islands as Mr. Roosevelt died, and the cause he represented and led was nearing the conclusive phase of success.

Less than two hours after the official announcement, Harry S. Truman of Missouri, the Vice President, took the oath as the thirty-second President. The oath was administered by the Chief Justice of the United States, Harlan F. Stone, in a one-minute ceremony at the White House. Mr. Truman immediately let it be known that Mr. Roosevelt's Cabinet is remaining in office and that he had authorized Secretary of State Edward R. Stettinius Jr. to proceed with plans for the United Nations Conference on international organization at San Francisco, scheduled to begin April 25. A report was circulated that

TRUMAN IS SWORN IN THE WHITE HOUSE

Members of Cabinet on Hand as Chief Justice Stone Administers the Oath

By C. P. TRUSSELL

WASHINGTON, April 12—Vice President Harry S. Truman of Missouri, standing erect, with his sharp features taut and looking straight ahead through his large, round glasses, became the thirty-

Afterword

In the process of assembling these pages, I've come to realize that tracing the life of a man like Franklin Delano Roosevelt is akin to throwing a stone into a pond and attempting to chart the ripples. The source is obvious enough, but as the concentric circles spin out from the origin, the wavelets mesh and intermingle though time and space until ultimately the only record of their passage is a gentle lapping against the shore. Eventually even this falls silent, and ultimately the hapless historian is left to draw his or her own conclusions of their original strength and direction. In the case of our 32nd president however, the remarkable fact is that more than 130 years after his birth, the force of that first throw, the sheer historical impetus of the man, remains so potent that these waves can still be felt today — an astounding vitality that is perhaps the most singular aspect of FDR's legacy.

For while these days Washington seems to worry solely about the politics of the moment — how a particular sound byte will play out, or how much the latest popularity poll has moved up or down, Franklin Roosevelt took the long view of governance. He realized full well that his New Deal policies would be unpopular in many circles — some wildly so — and he knew he risked his political future by implementing them. But he was less concerned with partisan politics or personal success than he was with the success of the country as a whole. His policies had the dual goal of not only ending the immediate economic crisis but also of making American society a less risky place in the future, mitigating what FDR called the "hazards and vicissitudes" of life.

The enduring alphabet soup of agencies he created, the FDIC, the SEC, the NLRB, the FHA shared the common goal of stabilizing current conditions while providing a foundation for solid, secure growth. None of these policies came without risk, political or otherwise. FDR understood, for instance, that his Social Security proposal would be an economic drag in the short run: the new payroll tax the president insisted on to fund the program was an additional burden that would place further stress on an already stressed economy. But he also realized that if he were ever to break the cycle of poverty amongst the infirm and aged, he needed to act now for the long term: "If, as our Constitution tells us," he said, "our Federal Government was established among other things 'to promote the general welfare,' it is our plain duty to provide for that security upon which welfare depends."

On the domestic front, examples of Roosevelt's far-sighted policies abound. We've already mentioned the public work projects of the CCC and WPA, which were widely attacked at the time as unwarranted

The shacks of the Bonus Army veterans burn in Washington after Hoover orders the military to forcibly remove them, July 1932.

government interference in the private sector, yet 80 years later still serve the common weal. Another is the G.I. Bill of Rights, perhaps the most lauded piece of veterans' legislation ever. Roosevelt had been a first-hand witness to the huge personal and economic dislocation caused by the return of the WWI veterans, which culminated in the march of the famous Bonus Army on Washington in 1932. Though that crisis was later defused — mostly by offering unemployed WWI veterans work in the CCC — the country had come close to armed revolt, and FDR determined that when "his boys" came home, they would face a better deal. Roosevelt threw his weight behind, and ultimately signed, legislation that provided for veteran preference in hiring; full tuition and expenses for education from grade to graduate school; and subsidized loans for veterans to invest in small businesses, farms and homes. Later, medical benefits were added. It's hard to underestimate the effect that the G.I. Bill had on American society, especially in terms of social mobility. For the very first time, members of all economic classes found entrée to areas previously reserved for the wealthy: access to banking services, quality health care and higher education. This road map to the future provided for the most successful integration of veterans in American history, and did much to lay the foundation for the economic prosperity that followed in the 50s and 60s.

Internationally, even FDR's harshest congressional critics grudgingly admitted that he was a superb wartime president, on a par with Washington or Lincoln. Roosevelt was an innate tactician, long experienced in military management, who understood both the global strategic situation, and the logistics required to win it. America's victory against Germany and Japan can largely be credited to the military balancing act that was, in essence, FDR's creation: the commitment to first conquer the spreading threat of Nazism in Europe, and then turn to the menace of Japan. This decision, the subject of bitter debate among FDR's advisors, must have been particularly tearing for the president. As a former assistant secretary of the navy, FDR's heart and soul were with his men at sea, and he knew that placing a secondary emphasis on the Pacific theater meant subjecting his beloved naval forces to years in harm's way as they attempted to stem the Japanese tide. Nevertheless, he did it, because he knew that if Britain fell, Hitler's dream of "Fortress Europe" would be come a reality, creating an armed monstrosity so mighty as to be impossible to dislodge. In hindsight, this decision probably saved the country. Had Germany had the time to complete its heavy water experiments and combine the result with its superior rocket technology, the war might easily have end-

1946: Eleanor Roosevelt addressing the United Nations, London. Following FDR's death, Eleanor remained active in politics for the rest of her life. President Harry Truman appointed her to the first United States delegation to the United Nations where she served as the chair of the Commission on Human Rights, and oversaw the drafting of the Universal Declaration of Human Rights. Later she chaired the Kennedy administration's Presidential Commission on the Status of Women.

ed very differently, with cataclysmic consequences for the United States and the world.

Yet even during the darkest years of the conflict, with Britain teetering under air assault and the Japanese extending their bloody path across the Pacific, one man was thinking about America's future *after* the War. It's impossible to know whether, in his heart of hearts, FDR ever seriously contemplated a United States defeat. His actions, though, would seem to indicate that he did not, for almost from the inception of hostilities, this remarkable intellect began to plan a new order of things, one in which America would not slip back into its isolationist past, but rather move forth in the company of other nations to create not just a better country, but a better world. Dragging his increasingly feeble frame to conference after conference in far-flung corners of the globe, FDR began, with Churchill (and a very reluctant Stalin) to formulate plans for a new organization that would work, if not to prevent, at least to mitigate the armed crises of the past. FDR articulated this shockingly simple philosophy in his last inaugural address, a mere few months before his death:

"Today, in this year of war, 1945, we have learned lessons — at a fearful cost — and we shall profit by them. We have learned that we cannot live alone, at peace; that our own well-being is dependent on the well-being of other nations, far away... We have learned to be citizens of the world, members of the human community. We have learned the simple truth, as Emerson said, that, 'The only way to have a friend is to be one.'"

Eighty years later, his dream endures, and the power of FDR's call still resonates.

Now all that's required of us is to answer it.

MICHAEL WEISHAN

1960: The tireless champion of the people carrying her own bags at LaGuardia Airport. Eleanor Roosevelt would die two years later at age 78.

Into the Future

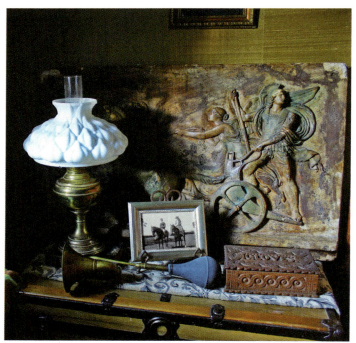
A classical frieze sits atop the steamer trunk in Lathrop's bedroom.

The FDR Suite Foundation at Adams House, Harvard College, was founded by a group of volunteer alumni in 2008. Its goal was ambitious: to return the Roosevelt rooms in Westmorly Hall to a semblance of their 1904 appearance as a museum and living memorial to the 32nd president — the only one at Harvard. This was accomplished after a six-year, quarter-million dollar restoration.

In addition to the Suite's museum function, the rooms also serve as the physical and spiritual headquarters of the Foundation's numerous educational programs. In addition to continuing research on FDR and the Harvard of 1904, work is underway on an Internet museum that will allow visitors to tour the Suite on-line and learn more about the long-lost world of Harvard's famed Gold Coast. Additionally, the Foundation sponsors various educational programs, including historical walking tours, documentary film productions, and an annual public lecture series, *The FDR Memorial Lecture*, which brings some of the nation's top historians and authors to speak at Adams House. Finally, the Foundation sponsors several scholarship programs, including an undergraduate summer study initiative, *The FDR Global Fellowship* program.

For more information about the Foundation and how you can help, please visit: www.fdrsuite.org.

The study looking toward the French doors from the entrance.

Atop the restored piano, 'Johnny' the bobcat forever vanquishes 'Eli' the quail, with Lathrop's bedroom beyond.

Late afternoon sunlight plays over FDR's rolltop desk.

It's forever May 1904 in the Suite; here FDR's boater patiently awaits his return.

The clutter of upper-class Victorian Harvard: polo mallets, golf clubs, fishing reels and a purloined bar sign in Lathrop's bedroom.

Lathrop's desk in the main study.

The sonorous coffin clock on the mantle sounds tea.

Photo Credits

The images in this book come courtesy of the FDR Presidential Library and Museum, with the following exceptions:

1900 Westmorly, The FDR Suite Foundation, Inc.
1901 Social whirl, Harvard University Archives/FDR Suite Foundation, Inc.
1903 Harvard/Yale The FDR Suite Foundation, Inc.
1903 Groton, The Family of Lathrop Brown
1915 On board ship, The Family of Lathrop Brown
1929 Market crash, National Archives
1932 Bonus Army, National Archives
1932 NYC Breadline, Dorothea Lange, National Archives
1932 Happy Days, The FDR Suite Foundation
1933 Bank Closure, WPA Images
1933 Beer, National Archives
1933 Sailing, National Archives
1933 CCC, University of Oregon Digital Archives
1934 Dustbowl, Farm Service Administration, National Archives
1937 Supreme Court, National Archives, Library of Congress
1939 *St. Louis*, National Archives
1939 Germany Invades, National Archives
1940 Election, Digital Collections of the State of Tennessee
1940 London, National Archives
1941 Pearl Harbor, National Archives
1943 Assembly plant, National Archives
1944 Normandy, National Archives
1944 Japanese Internment, Dorothea Lange, National Archives
1945 A Nation Mourns, The New York Times
2013 The FDR Suite, The FDR Suite Foundation, Inc & Ralph Lieberman

Acknowledgments

• Dr. Cynthia Koch, former Director of the FDR Presidential Library and Museum, for her friendship, encouragement, and advice.

• Claire Mays '81, for her keen editorial eye.

• Drs. Judy and Sean Palfrey, Masters of Adams House, for their constant support and enthusiasm.

• The FDR Presidential Library and Museum, and all their staff for patiently enduring my hundreds of requests.

• The Reverend George Salzmann, the treasurer of our Foundation and fellow FDR enthusiast, for his calm guidance.

• And finally, grateful thanks to all those whose financial assistance made this book possible, in particular the Lillian Goldman Charitable Trust for its major funding of the FDR Suite Restoration, and the Friends of the FDR Suite Foundation.

Made in the USA
Charleston, SC
23 September 2013